# Dare to Care!

By Jenny Alexander

Consultant Dr. Alice Brown DEdPsy, CPsychol

ARCTURUS

This edition published in 2022 by Arcturus Publishing Limited
26/27 Bickels Yard, 151–153 Bermondsey Street,
London SE1 3HA

Copyright © Arcturus Holdings Limited

All rights reserved. No part of this publication may be reproduced, stored in a retrieval system, or transmitted, in any form or by any means, electronic, mechanical, photocopying, recording, or otherwise, without prior written permission in accordance with the provisions of the Copyright Act 1956 (as amended). Any person or persons who do any unauthorized act in relation to this publication may be liable to criminal prosecution and civil claims for damages.

Author: Jenny Alexander
Consultant: Dr. Alice Brown DEdPsy, CPsychol
Illustrator: Valentina Jaskina
Designer: Nathan Balsom
Editor: Becca Clunes
Managing Designer: Jessica Holliland
Managing Editor: Joe Harris

ISBN: 978-1-3988-2025-8
CH010090NT
Supplier 29, Date 0822, PI 00002215

Printed in China

# Contents

# Do you dare to care?

Kindness is like an invisible hug that connects us with other people. It feels comforting to know that someone cares about us, and we want to pass that feeling on, but sometimes we might feel scared to care.

Kindness means thinking about other people's feelings, helping each other, and trying not to do things that could hurt someone. It makes our world feel warm and safe. We have chances to be kind every day, but sometimes we might hold back.

We might be worried in case they don't want our help. They might push us away. Or we might think, "I'm just a kid. What difference can I make?" Or we might get caught up in our own little world and forget to make the time to help other people.

Maybe we have made mistakes in the past and hurt someone's feelings without meaning to. Then we might think that there's no point in trying, because we just aren't a kind person. Or maybe some of the people around us think kindness is not important—or even that it is a weakness.

But kindness is a strength. It is a skill that we can work at and get good at. The more we do it, the easier it gets. Also, the more we do it, the more we want to, because caring for others makes us feel good about ourselves.

This book is full of ideas that can help you dare to care.

### Who can help

Everyone! People who do kind things can give you ideas about what you could do to be kind, and people who do unkind things can show you what you don't want to do. You can talk about the ideas in this book with a trusted family member or friend, and they can join in with some of the activities if they want to. Sharing is caring!

# Think big

When it comes to caring, don't just think about the people you love—everything you care about builds up your ability to be kind.

Caring isn't just about being kind to the people you love or even just the people you know. You can be kind to strangers.

It isn't just about people, either. You can care about pets and other animals.

You can care about plants and trees and all of nature.

You can care about your home and your local area
You can care about the whole world!

Draw the people and things
you can show kindness to.

- Pink—Put yourself in the middle with
  your family and friends.

- Yellow—Add some strangers in the
  yellow circle.

- Green—Now draw animals, birds, and
  fish in the green circle.

- Blue—Fill in the blue circle with
  flowers and trees.

### How it helps

Caring about people and things outside your close
family and friends helps you build your skills and
see yourself as a caring, kind of person.

# You have the power!

Imagine there was a superpower that could make the whole world happier. Well, there is, and it is kindness.

You don't have to be kind. It's your choice, and it isn't always easy. Do you have the power to choose kindness? Do this *little* test and find out.

Shade in the squares to show how well you think you do.

1. I try to make people happy.

    Never    Rarely    Sometimes    Often    Always

2. I help out when I'm asked.

    Never    Rarely    Sometimes    Often    Always

3. I show that everybody matters.

    Never    Rarely    Sometimes    Often    Always

4. I try to make a difference.

    Never    Rarely    Sometimes    Often    Always

## Results.

If you marked "sometimes" or "often," then you are using your superpower. Keep up the good work!

If you marked "never" or "rarely," then keep trying. You have the power, because everybody does.

If you marked "always," think again. Nobody is perfect all the time!

Claim your power now by putting your name on your certificate.
Add more stars to make the frame look bright and beautiful.

## Certificate

Right now,

.........................................................

is a kind and caring person.

### How it helps

Choosing to see yourself as a kind person right now is a way of claiming the natural power that we all have to make the world a better place.

# Happy mind, happy body

Caring makes us feel good, not just in our emotions but in our bodies, too. Do this little experiment to feel how it works.

When we are upset or unhappy, we might say, "Go away!" and "I don't care!" Try it now. Imagine that something has upset you—maybe someone has said a mean thing, or you got told off for something you didn't do. You feel upset and angry. Shut your eyes so you can really imagine it.

I don't care!

What is happening in your body? Are your muscles getting tight? Are your shoulders hunching? Is your head tilting down? What is happening in your face? Notice your breathing.

Hold that position for 30 seconds, then let it go. Shake your feet, shake your hands—take a deep breath in and sigh it out.

Now close your eyes again, and imagine that you have just done something kind for someone else. They are thanking you, and you are glad you could help. Feel the emotions and notice what is happening in your body.

Are your muscles softening? Are your shoulders back? Is your head up? What is happening in your face? Notice your breathing.

Feel how kindness, even when you're just imagining it, can give your body a boost.

### How it helps

Caring is good for your body because it makes you feel happy, and happiness releases chemicals in your brain that relax your muscles and steady your heartbeat and breathing.

# If you wouldn't say it to their face ...

When you are talking about other people, there is a simple kindness rule. If you wouldn't say it to their face, don't say it behind their back.

Sometimes people are mean about someone behind their back, and you might be tempted to join in. You might think, "What's the problem? They can't hear us. They will never know!"

But that makes it worse. You are not only being mean behind their back, you are also tricking them by hiding what you really think. If they don't know what people are saying about them, they can't say anything back, and that isn't fair.

So, when people are whispering behind someone's back, don't join in. You are not being unfriendly—you are being true to yourself as the kind person you are.

Not joining in tells everyone you don't think it's all right to gossip behind someone's back. That could make other people start to feel that it isn't all right, too, and then they might stop gossiping.

When your friends notice that you never join in with unkind gossiping, they will know they can trust you never to say mean things about them behind their back.

### How it helps

When you don't join in with saying unkind things behind someone's back, you are not only sticking up for them but also for yourself. Not joining in tells everyone that you are a kind and trustworthy person.

# Hello, people!

Would you like to send kind thoughts out into the world
for people you will never even meet? Well, you can!

Collect some smooth stones—they can be round or flat. You will need some acrylic paints or pens. (Acrylic just means that they are made of plastics and won't wash away in the rain.)

Have a nice day!

Write the messages you want to send to other people. Some of your stones could just have pictures.

Place your stones where people passing by will see them. You might make someone's day!

### How it helps

Science shows that kindness always makes us feel good, but that isn't only because other people see you and say thank you. Even if nobody knows it was you, doing a kind thing still gives you a happiness boost.

# Spot it, stop it

You can be unkind to yourself without even noticing.
Here's how to spot it and stop it.

Being kind to the people you love is easy.
Being kind to people you don't really like is
harder. But sometimes the hardest thing of
all is being kind to yourself.

Almost everyone thinks unkind
thoughts about themselves from
time to time. Things like, "I'm
so stupid" or "Nobody likes
me." Thinking unkind thoughts
about yourself is so common
that it has a name. It's
called "beating yourself up."

**What unkind things do
you sometimes think
about yourself?**

_____

_____

_____

_____

Look at each one and ask, "Is that what someone kind would say?"

Are you really a stupid person, or do you just sometimes make a mistake? Everybody makes mistakes! Is there really not a single person in the world who likes you, or is it just that there a few people who don't?

When it comes to the mean thoughts on your list, what could you say to yourself instead? Imagine that it was someone you love saying those things about themselves. What would you say to them?

Every time you notice that you are beating yourself up, stop and think about it. Find something kind to say instead.

_____

_____

_____

_____

### Why it helps

Having unkind thoughts about yourself makes you feel unhappy and doesn't do any good. Stopping it is being kind to yourself.

# Story magic

There are lots of fairy tales where an act of kindness can break
a wicked spell. Here is one—the story of the frog in the well.

Read the story, and
fill in the pictures.

A princess was playing with a golden ball. It fell into a well.

A frog said, "I will get it for you, if you will be my friend."

The frog found the ball, but the princess ran away. "I don't want to be friends with a FROG!" she said.

The frog was very sad. The princess came back.

"Don't cry," she said.

The princess kissed the frog on the head.

The frog turned into a prince. "There was a spell on me. Only the kindness of a princess could break it," he said.

## How it helps

Fairy tales have magic, but they also say something important about real life. The story of the frog in the well shows how being kind can turn a stranger into a friend.

# Care for your local area

Wherever you live, you can help keep your local area clean and tidy,
and that makes life better for everyone.

Nobody would drop their empty food packages and plastic bottles on their own doorstep, because it would make their home look messy and uncared for.

But some people do drop their litter in the street or on the beach, or in parks and public spaces. They don't care what it feels like for the people who live there. You can care!

No one can keep the whole world clean and tidy, but everyone can help take care of their local area.

Here are some ideas

- Get together with family members or friends, and do a litter pickup around your local streets.

- Have a competition to see who can pick up the most pieces of litter.

- Ask your teacher if you can organise a litter pick up around your school.

- Look for organized litter-picking events, such as cleaning a beach, that you could join in with.

- Join a group that organizes litter-picking locally.

Notice how caring for the environment brings people together.

## Litter pick up here today!
### Let's keep our park tidy.

Litter can be dangerous for animals. If we keep our park clean, then we can all play our part in looking after nature.

**Litter-pickers and gloves provided!**

**Bring a picnic, and stay for some ball games afterward.**

### How it helps

Caring for your local area is a way of caring for all the people who live there, making it nice for them as well as for yourself.

# It's only a joke!

Teasing and silly nicknames are often just a little fun between friends.
But if you are not careful, they can be hurtful.

Have you ever felt upset when someone teased you or called
you by a nickname? If you complained, they probably said,
"Don't be silly. It's only a joke!"

But it isn't a joke if people go on teasing
and name-calling when they know it's making
someone feel upset. It is bullying.

If you have said something that upset someone, even though you thought you were being funny, simply say sorry and stop doing it.

Sometimes people will try not to show that they feel upset because they don't want to look like they can't take a joke. So how can you be sure your that teasing and name-calling is fun and not unkind?

Think about things you have said in teasing. If you said those things seriously, how would they make the person feel? If you wouldn't say it in a serious voice, it's safer not to say it at all.

### How it helps

Words can hurt. Being aware that teasing and name-calling isn't always funny for the person who is being teased can help us avoid being unkind without meaning to.

# Find your passion

Everything you care about builds up your caring abilities,
and that includes the activities you love to do.

In your free time, when you can choose, what do you like to do? Maybe you love making things or writing stories—or playing sports, or cooking, or dancing. It doesn't matter which hobbies you choose—one isn't better than another. The important thing is that you really enjoy it.

When you are doing something you really enjoy, you don't notice the time going by or the things happening around you. This is called "being in the flow."

What things do you love doing in your free time?

_____

_____

_____

_____

What things do you think you might love doing, but you haven't tried them yet?

_____

_____

_____

_____

Think about joining clubs or classes where you might meet other people who share your interests.

## How it helps

Doing things you enjoy gives you a happiness boost, so it is an important part of caring for yourself. It also allows you to give something your full attention and take your time, which are two great caring skills.

# Just listen

Sometimes what people need is just to talk to someone,
so one of the most important kindness skills is knowing how to listen.

Are you a good listener? Not everyone is, because not everyone knows the rules. Listening is important when someone wants to talk about something that is worrying or upsetting them.

### Rule 1
### Put your own feelings aside

Stop what you're doing, and give your friend your full attention. You might think differently from them, but try not to let your thoughts and feelings keep you from hearing how your friend thinks and feels about the situation.

### Rule 2
### Just listen

You are only half listening if you are thinking all the time about what you are going to say next. Don't worry about what you are going to say. Give your full attention to your friend.

### Rule 3
### Try and understand the problem

Your job is to try and understand the problem. You don't have to come up with a solution.

When someone wants to talk about a problem, they just need you to hear them and understand how they are feeling. Listen, and let them know you think their feelings matter by saying something like, "That must be very worrying" or "I'm sorry that you are upset." That is often enough to make them feel better.

### How it helps

The point of talking isn't always to try and figure out what to do. Just talking and being listened to can make people feel cared for and comforted.

# Make a non-birthday cake

Have you heard of "random acts of kindness"? It just means doing something nice for someone when they aren't expecting it. No one expects to have a cake made specially for them when it isn't their birthday!

Who would you like to surprise with a non-birthday cake? It might be a friend or a family member. Who could you get to help you?

If you have never made a cake before, use a box of cake mix and follow the instructions. If you know how to make a cake from a cookbook, you can do that. Whichever way you do it, making cakes is fun!

How can you make the cake special? Could you write the person's name in chocolate chips or raisins? Could you make a little flag with a cocktail stick and write a message on it? Have you got some edible decorations?

Best friend!

Good going

When you give your cake to the person, tell them, "This is just because you are a good friend," or whatever your special message is. Enjoy surprising them with this random act of kindness.

Make a plan for your cake here.

### How it helps

We all make or buy things for our family and friends on their birthdays. Making a non-birthday cake is a way of remembering that we don't have to wait for a special occasion to do lovely things for each other.

# When you mess up

Nobody's perfect, and you are bound to make mistakes. But when you make a mistake, you can make it better by simply saying sorry.

Sometimes we *all* can say something
unkind without thinking or not notice
when somebody needs our help,
especially when we feel tired or upset.

When that happens, the best thing to do is simply to say sorry.

If possible, when you have said sorry, try and think of a way to show that you mean it.

When you have said sorry and shown that you mean it, you can let it go. There is no point in worrying about it anymore, because you have done everything you can to make it better. If you find it hard to let go of your worries, you might want to talk to an adult you trust about it.

## How it helps

Saying sorry to someone shows them that you know you were unkind, and you feel bad about it. That helps you both to feel better about what happened and move on.

# Really look

When was the last time you really looked at yourself?
You might have forgotten this, but you are amazing!

Albert Einstein was one of the cleverest people who ever lived, and he said that there were two ways of looking at the world. You could either see it as if everything was amazing, or else see it as if nothing was.

But if you really look, then there is only one way. Everything is amazing!

Look at yourself in the mirror. Take your time. Look at your hair, the way it grows from your head. Look at your forehead, your nose, your mouth, your bright and wonderful eyes.

Now draw a picture of yourself here. When you draw from life—making pictures of real things and the people you can see in front of you—that makes you really look.

When you draw yourself, notice how amazing you are. You are worth caring about, so always remember to be caring and kind to yourself.

## How it helps

Sometimes we only see our faults. Really noticing how amazing we are helps keep us from having unkind thoughts about ourselves.

# The starfish story

Do you sometimes think you are too young to make a difference?
This famous story could make you think again.

A child was walking along a sandy beach. Thousands of starfish had been washed up onto the sand, and she was throwing them back into the sea.

A man asked her, "Why are you doing that?"

She explained that the starfish would die if they stayed too long out of the water.

"But the beach goes on for miles, and there are millions of starfish," said the man. "Putting a few back in the water won't make any difference."

The child looked at the starfish in her hand.

"It makes a difference to this one," she said, as she threw it into the waves.

The man slowly nodded his head. He called to his family and friends, and they all started to help the girl. Soon, everyone on the beach was joining in, and hundreds of starfish that would have died were saved.

## How it helps

Any time you think that small things don't make a difference, remember the starfish story. Every kind thing you do for someone makes a difference to that person and encourages other people to be kind as well.

How many starfish can you rescue by copying them from the sand into the water?

# Hug a tree, plant a tree

Being kind to people is important, but we should also remember to be kind to the natural world.

Trees are our friends. They shelter us from the wind and rain and give us shade on a hot day. They take pollution out of the air and produce the oxygen we need to survive. It isn't surprising that hugging a tree releases happiness chemicals in the brain.

Try it and see. Hug some different kinds of trees. Is there one you like best?

If it is the right time of year, you might notice the seeds of the tree scattered on the ground underneath it.

Help them grow over a wider area by picking some up and planting them in another spot. Dig a shallow hole with a stick, drop the seed in, and cover it with soil.

In nature, seeds are spread over a wide area by animals and birds, or they're blown by the wind or washed away to other places by streams and rivers.

You can be part of the team and do your best for nature.

### How it helps

Hugging a tree makes us feel calmer and more connected with nature. Planting a tree is a generous thing to do because trees grow very slowly. They are a gift to people who will come after us in the future.

# Let other people be kind to you

People like to be able to help, so don't be afraid to ask.

We all need a helping hand sometimes. You might need help with a practical problem such as learning a new game or understanding your schoolwork. You might need to talk things through with someone, or sometimes you might just need a cuddle.

It can be difficult to ask for help when you need it because you might feel shy or silly. You might think you're too grown up to ask for help and that you should be able to manage on your own.

But most people are happy to help. It makes them feel good. So, you asking them is good for them, too.

Because people do like to help, sometimes someone might do something for you when you didn't ask. They might say something nice about your new coat, ask if you would like to play, or offer to share their sandwich with you.

The kind thing then is to smile and say thank you, even if you feel embarrassed that they commented on your coat, or you don't want to play, or you think their sandwich looks disgusting. You don't have to play or eat the sandwich—it's just nice to make them feel glad they offered.

### How it helps

Being able to ask for help is a kindness, because you are giving someone else the opportunity to be kind. So is saying thank you when someone offers even though you didn't ask, because it makes them feel good about offering.

# Play "stuck in the mud"

Sometimes you might miss an opportunity to be kind because you didn't notice that someone needed help. Exercise your noticing skills and have fun playing "stuck in the mud."

## How to play

One person is the catcher, and everyone else runs away. When the catcher touches someone, they must stand still with their arms out and their legs apart as if they are stuck in the mud.

Any player who is still free can rescue the ones who are stuck in the mud by crawling through their legs. If the catcher can get all the other players stuck in the mud, they win.

The last person to be tagged becomes the catcher. Then everyone else runs away, as the game begins again.

To be good at this game, you need to watch your team to see who needs help. You'll soon discover that if you make sure your friends escape, they will make an effort to free you if you get stuck in the mud yourself.

### How it helps
Games like "stuck in the mud" remind us that helping other people can be fun.

# Kings and queens of kind

Who cares about you? Who is kind to you? Who could you go to if you needed help?
Crown your own kings and queens of kind!

Write down some of the people who are kind to you. Try to include friends, family, people you see every day, and people you don't know very well.

_____

_____

_____

_____

_____

Make some of these people your kings and queens of kind.

Write their name and how they are kind. Would they like red or blue or green or yellow or purple or pink for their crown?

Mr. Dolan in the school office. He always asks me, "How are you today?"

## How it helps

It is easy to take the people who are kind to you for granted and forget how important they are. Their kindness makes the world feel safe and shows you how to be a caring person.

# "I will not judge today!"

Everyone has problems and worries they keep to themselves.
You never know what's going on for anyone else, so just be kind.

Have you ever felt upset or worried but tried to hide it?
We all do that sometimes.

Here are Finn, Kayla, and Joaquim on their way to school. Two of them are feeling worried or upset. Can you tell which two?

Finn is worried he's going to fail his test. Kayla is upset because her parents had an argument this morning. Joaquim is having a good day! You can't always tell how someone is feeling by the way they look.

We don't always show our feelings. The unfriendly boy in your class might just be very shy. Your teacher's bad mood this week might be because her dog is sick, and she feels worried about him. The new girl who didn't thank you when you helped her find her class might not be used to people being kind to her, and she may not know what to say.

Instead of thinking, "Why should I be kind to him, when he never speaks to me?" you could think, "He never speaks to me, I wonder if he has any friends? Maybe I should say hello at lunchtime and ask if he wants to play a game."

Sometimes the people who are uncomfortable or in a bad mood are the ones who need kindness the most.

### How it helps

Understanding that you don't know what other people are going through means you can be kind to everyone.

# Better together

Things work better when we help each other.
That's the secret of our success!

Human beings are social animals. It's in our nature to help one another, and being able to work together is what makes us so successful as a species.

Think how many people working together it took to make this book.

bookstore worker

writer

illustrator

delivery truck driver

printer

workers growing trees
to make paper

Think how many people it took to make you into a reader! Fill in the pictures.

reading baby
books to you

teaching you
the alphabet

helping you read
longer books

sharing and
swapping

running the
library

What skills and interests could you share with
other people? Maybe you love sports, or art,
or cooking. Could you join a club or see if your
friends would like to do it with you?

### How it helps

We can do a lot of things on our own, but
we can do more when we do it together!

# Don't be a bystander

Is someone at school being picked on?
Don't just stand by and watch it happen.

If someone is being picked on and you do nothing—or even worse, you join in, you're letting everyone think that you believe it's all right to be unkind.

You don't have to be their best friend, but when somebody is being bullied, a simple act of kindness could make a big difference to them.

When other kids see that you never join in with bullying, that could make them think again before they do. If you can offer a kind word or helping hand to someone who is being bullied, you may also inspire other kids to do the same. This is how to make the world a kinder place.

### How it helps

Being kind to someone when other people are being mean makes them feel better, and it can also encourage others not to just stand by and watch it happen, too.

# Make a kindness collage

Art is a fun way of celebrating the good things, and kindness is a very good thing. Celebrate with your friends and family by making a kindness collage.

Here is a kindness collage.

What you will need:

- A glue stick
- Some different kinds of paper
- A magazine

I helped Marcus with his homework.

Ms. Solis gave me a "Congratulations" sticker.

Sara and I took her dog for a walk.

Albert let me go first when we played a game.

Add pictures from magazines if you like.

Give your friends and family small pieces of paper, and ask them to write down some kind things they did or kind things someone did for them. Glue them on this page. Add some pictures from magazines to make your collage brighter.

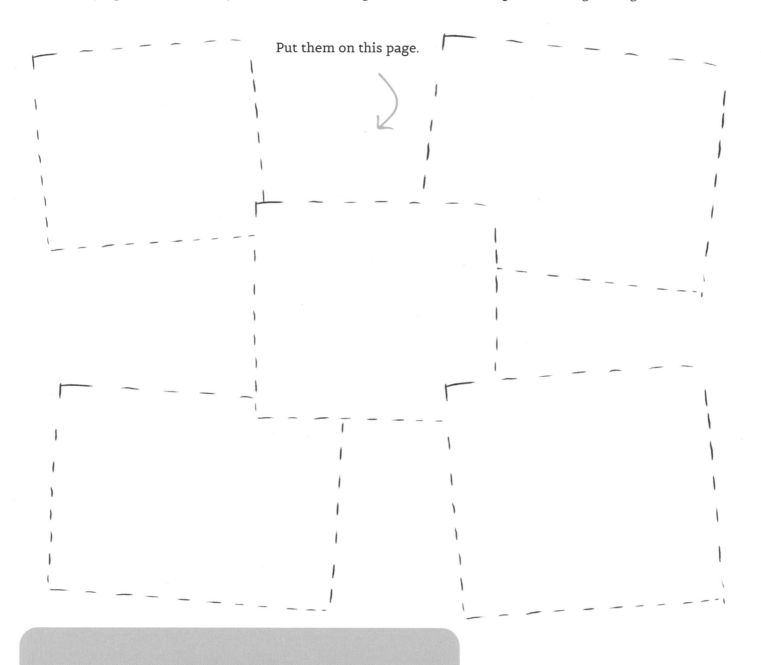

Put them on this page.

### How it helps

Making art is a great way of celebrating kindness. Doing it together means that we can celebrate and inspire each other.

# Play nice!

Playing board games is fun, but only if everyone plays nicely.
That means caring about other people's feelings as well as your own.

If you're winning, remember to be kind to the other players. Don't tease them, or they might feel annoyed.

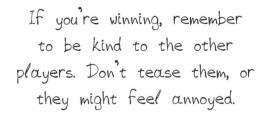

If you're losing, you might want to sulk, stop playing, or throw the board up in the air. The other players would not feel happy about that!

You are bound to feel glad if you are winning and sad if you are losing. Being a good sport means not letting your own feelings spoil the other players' fun.

### How it helps

Playing board games is a great way of learning how to notice and care about other people's feelings, because we enjoy ourselves better if everyone is having a good time.

# How was your day?

When someone asks you, "How was your day?" they are showing that they care about you. But do you sometimes not know what to say?

People don't ask, "What happened in your day today?" but "How was your day?"

What matters isn't just the things that happened but also how you felt about them.

Think about your day today. Maybe there wasn't any juice at breakfast time, and you felt cross. Or maybe your best friend was waiting for you when you got to school, and you felt happy.

Make a list of things that happened and how you felt about them.

My day today

Now write the story of your day here.

If you prefer, you could draw a picture of something that happened, showing how you felt about it in your face.

### How it helps

Writing about your day in words or pictures helps you think about your feelings. You will know what to say if you're asked the question "How was your day?"

# Look after your body

Do you ever think about your body
apart from when you are sick? What do you say?

Our bodies are amazing! But if we ever think about them at all, we often say critical things like "My legs are too short" or "My tummy is too big" or "I don't like my nose!"

Show your body some love by taking a minute to notice just how wonderful it is. Lie down, close your eyes, and think about all the things your body is doing right now.

Your heart is pumping blood, your lungs are helping you breathe, and your stomach is digesting food. All your organs are working together to keep your body healthy, and your brain is running everything, making sure that they never stop doing their job.

Think about your skin and your ears, eyes, and nose. They help you feel, hear, see, smell, and taste.

Say thank you to your body. Promise that you will say and think positive things about it every day.

Look after your body by choosing foods that help it keep fit and healthy. You don't always have a choice but when you do, sometimes choose the fruit instead of the sweet desert, and have a slice of toast instead of chocolate and salty snacks.

Foods I love, but my body doesn't like

Foods my body loves

(Clue: These are the ones that are super sweet or salty!)

## How it helps

Looking after your body is part of looking after yourself.

# Try exercise snacking!

Your body needs exercise, but what if you don't like sports?
Don't worry. You can look after your body in lots of different ways.

You know that looking after your body includes getting enough exercise. But what if you hate sports or you can't go to the park very often?

The good news is that the experts say five little sessions of exercise every day might be even better for your body than a whole session in the gym or on a playing field a few times a week. They call it "exercise snacking."

Exercise snacks are five to ten minutes of any activity that makes your heart beat faster, such as:

- Putting on some music and dancing

- Going up and down the stairs

- Doing some star jumps

- Running on the spot during commercials on TV

What other exercise snacks can you think of in your normal life? If you live on the fourth floor, maybe you could walk up the stairs instead of taking the elevator. At school, you could ask your friends to play a game where you run around. Write some ideas:

_____

_____

_____

_____

The key to success, when it comes to exercise snacking, is not to avoid moving. Did you forget to bring your dirty plate down from your bedroom? Great! You get to run upstairs again! Do your parents need a hand bringing the shopping in? Awesome! That gets you up out of your seat. Did you hear the doorbell? Say, "I'll go!"

Don't see having to make an effort a pain. Instead, see it as an opportunity to give your body a treat.

### How it helps

Not enough exercise can make our bodies feel sluggish and affect our moods, and it's hard to care about anything when we feel tired and irritable.

# Smile!

Have you ever felt worried or upset, and then someone smiled at you and made you feel better? A smile is a little thing that can make a big difference.

Look at this sad face. How does it make you feel?

Now turn the book, and look at the picture the other way up. How does it make you feel now?

You can make someone feel better with a smile, so turn that frown upside down!

A smile says, "Hello, I see you, and I care about you. How are you today?" And when we smile at someone, even a stranger, they almost always smile back. Their smile seems to say, "I'm fine. Thank you for asking!"

Put some smiles on all these faces. Make them happy!

### How it helps

Smiling is an easy way to show you care. Your smile can cheer someone up, and when they smile back, their smile can cheer you up, too. Even when you are on your own, you can give yourself a little smile and feel a happiness boost.

# Remember to say

If you like something, don't be shy to say so!

Write down some things you liked.

Put a sunny smile in the boxes if you told the person that you liked it. If you didn't tell them at the time, you can still tell them now, and then you can put a smile in the box.

Something someone cooked for you

_____

☐

Something someone was wearing

_____

☐

A gift someone gave you

_____

☐

Someone's new look or hairstyle

_____

☐

Something someone made themselves

_____

☐

You never need to tell a lie and say you like something when you don't. You just need to remember to say so when you do.

It's the same if you don't like something. There's no need to lie. But it might be kinder not to say!

### How it helps

Saying when you like something is a simple act of kindness that makes people feel happy. It makes you happy, too, because it helps you notice all the good things you enjoy.

# Learn from your mistakes

Everyone makes mistakes, but that is normal. Mistakes are how we learn.

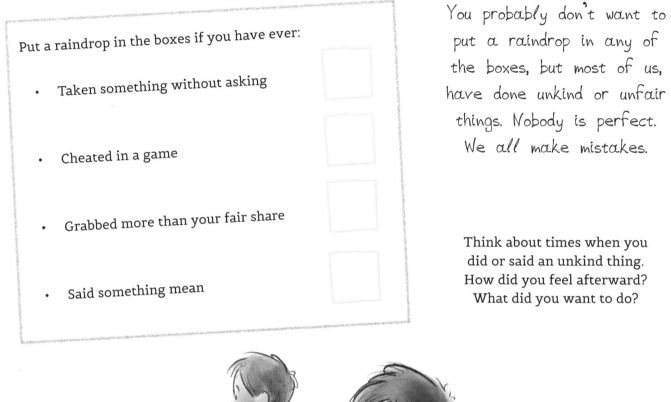

Put a raindrop in the boxes if you have ever:

- Taken something without asking

- Cheated in a game

- Grabbed more than your fair share

- Said something mean

You probably don't want to put a raindrop in any of the boxes, but most of us, have done unkind or unfair things. Nobody is perfect. We *all* make mistakes.

Think about times when you did or said an unkind thing. How did you feel afterward? What did you want to do?

If we have done something that made us feel bad, we remember that feeling, and it keeps us from doing it again. That's how we *learn* from our mistakes.

We learn from our successes, too. When we remember how good it feels to be nice to other people, we want to do it more.

Put a happy sun in the boxes if you have ever:

• Given someone a hug when they felt sad

• Said something kind

• Let someone share

• Offered to help

How did it make you feel? Would you like to feel that way again? You know what to do!

## How it helps

Part of being kind to yourself is accepting that you are bound to make mistakes. That is easier when you understand that every mistake is an opportunity to learn.

# Your own little piece of nature

Do you like being outside among plants and flowers?
Bring that feeling home by caring for an indoor plant.

Different plants have different needs. Some like to be in bright sunshine, but others prefer a shady spot. Some like to be watered often, others hardly at all.

No plant likes to stand in water all the time. Would you?

When you have an indoor plant to look after, you have to pay attention to its needs and notice what makes it stressed or happy.

Are the leaves droopy? Maybe it needs more water or perhaps you are watering it too much. If the leaves look scorched, your plant wants to be farther away from the window.

### How it helps

Caring for an indoor plant means noticing when it is not very happy and trying different ways of helping. It is just like caring for a person!

# A bunch of presents

Acts of kindness are gifts we give to each other.
Being grateful for them is a gift we give to ourselves.

Think about kind things other people have done for you. Write them on the gift tags. Then make the gifts look bright and beautiful.

Jay let me go first on the slide

Choose one, and write a thank you letter.

Dear _____

Thank you for _____

_____

_____

_____

_____

_____

_____

_____

_____

_____

_____

With love from _____

Have you noticed how feeling grateful makes you smile? Grateful feelings are a gift of kindness to yourself.

### How it helps

Noticing when people are kind to you makes you feel safe and loved. It can also give you ideas for ways that you can be kind to others.

# Touchy-feely

Sometimes you just want a hug, but what if
there's no trusted person around to hug you?

When you feel any strong emotion—say that you're super happy
or super sad or lonely—you might feel like having a hug, because
hugging calms your body and that is a way of calming your emotions.

You can get the calming effects of a hug even if there's no trusted
person around to give you one. Try hugging a pet, a cuddly toy, or a
pillow. Feel the way that holding them close to you calms your body.

Give yourself a hug! You could hum a soothing
tune to yourself as you do

Or pull a heavy blanket around you. See how its
warmth and heaviness settles you.

### How it helps

We can't always have a hug with someone we love, so it's good to
know that other kinds of hugs can also make us feel calm and happy.

# Make an imaginary pen pal

**Who would you like to tell your troubles to? Find the perfect person in your imagination!**

Imagine that there was someone you could talk to about anything. What would this person be like? Picture them in your mind. Maybe they are older and wiser, or maybe they are the same age as you.

Write down some things about them.

Name: _____

What they look like: _____

Where they live: _____

What they do for fun: _____

Close your eyes and really imagine them.

Dear _____

_____

_____

_____

_____

_____

_____

_____

With love from _____

Is anything bothering you today?
Write a letter!

Dear _____

_____

_____

_____

_____

_____

_____

_____

With love from _____

Then imagine what they would
say, and write a letter back
from them to you.

## How it helps

Talking about problems helps you understand how you are feeling. An
imaginary penfriend can help you find more ideas about how to make it better.

# The middle of the sandwich

What is the point of daring to care? It makes life better!

Think about bread. Maybe bread with a little butter on it. Two slices of bread.

Bread fills us up when we are hungry, and it tastes okay.

Now imagine making those two slices of bread into a sandwich.

What fillings would you add to your sandwich?
Does that make your slices of bread feel more interesting?

The two slices of bread are like two people. They are both perfectly fine on their own. Imagine that the filling is the caring that sticks them together. Bread is good, but a sandwich is better!

## How it helps

We might think that we ought to be able to manage on our own, and most of the time we can. Caring just makes life better.

# "They are not like us!"

### Everyone is different, but we all belong together.

Sometimes people may be unkind to others because they are different in some way. Maybe they have two mothers or two fathers, or they are super clever. They might have a disability, or a different religion, or come from a different country, or wear different kinds of clothes.

Although we are all different on the surface, underneath we are all the same. We all have hopes and dreams, sorrows and disappointments. We go through the same emotions.

Being unkind to people just because we think that they are different doesn't make sense. It keeps us separate and makes our life small. Kindness makes connections. It breaks down barriers and makes life feel bigger and more interesting.

Imagine that you were a red dot in a world made up of dots.

If you only cared about red dots, your world would be this big.

If you cared about all the dots, your world would look like this.

Draw some more dots with faces on this page.

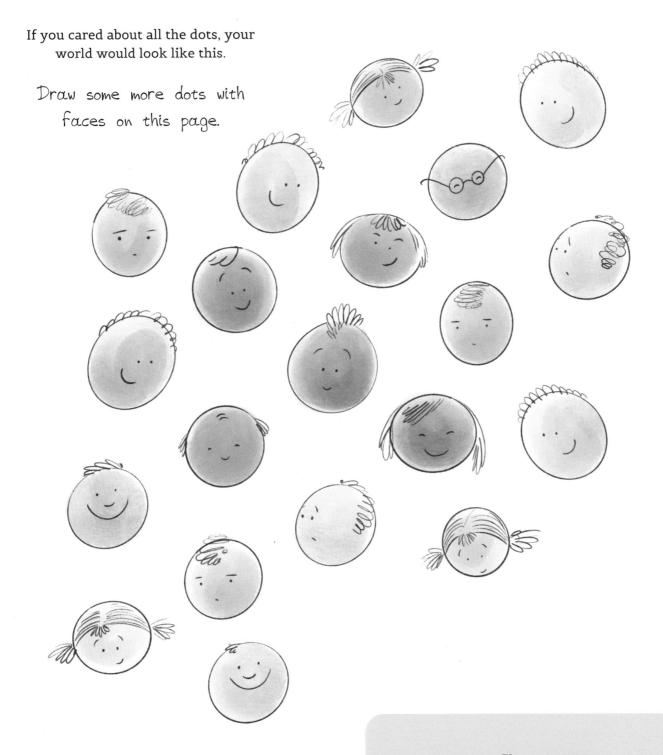

### How it helps

Caring about everyone, even people who seem different from yourself, gives you a happy feeling of belonging in one big human family.

# Are you forgetting someone?

Being kind should make you feel good. But what if it doesn't?

Being kind means thinking about other people and trying to make their life better, and the good news is that it makes your own life better, too. Caring for others makes you feel happy, and it's good for your self-esteem.

If it doesn't feel good, it might be that you're caring so much about other people that you are forgetting to care enough about yourself.

Always remember, every act of kindness is your choice. You should never feel that you have to be kind. If someone is being unkind to you, you do not have to be kind to them. If you always share, but the person you are sharing with does not share back, then you can choose to stop.

You don't have to be kind to make people like you or because people expect you to. You don't have to agree with everyone in order not to hurt their feelings or let other people take your kindness for granted.

If being kind to other people stops making you feel good, that means you need to boost your caring power by being extra kind to yourself.

When it comes to being kind, your feelings are the clue. If it makes you feel powerless and down, stop and take stock. If it makes you feel happy and good about yourself, you are on the right track—keep going!

### How it helps

Being kind to yourself is what gives you the energy to be kind to other people. It reminds you that your feelings matter, and kindness is your choice.

# Make a treasure hunt

Would you like to give something nice to your family and friends? You don't have to spend money. Give them your time instead by making a treasure hunt for them.

Everyone loves a treasure hunt! All you need is some paper, a pen, and a prize. Start by thinking of some places around your house where you could put a clue. Could you prop one up on a bookshelf, stick one under a refrigerator magnet, or place one on the front doormat? They need to be places where people can read them without having to move anything out of the way.

When you have thought of some good places, write the clues on small pieces of paper.

"Look beside a book!"

"Brrr … it's cold in here!"

"Knock, knock!"

Brrr… it's cold in here!

Put the clue on the place before, so the refrigerator one won't be on the refrigerator but on the bookshelf. Each clue tells everyone where to look next.

When all the clues are in place, gather the players together and give them the first clue. Enjoy watching them have fun trying to find all the others, until they get to the treasure at the end.

The treasure doesn't really matter. It can be something very small. The fun is in the race to find it.

You could do your treasure hunt outdoors if you have some outside space, so long as it's not wet or windy.

You found the treasure!

## How it helps

A gift doesn't have to cost money. You can give your time instead and create something special for other people.

# What's the worst that could happen?

Sometimes reaching out to other people can feel scary, especially if you are a very shy person or if you have been pushed away in the past. It can take courage to be kind, which is why this book is called *Dare to Care*.

When you hold back from doing something that you want to do out of fear, it always helps to ask, "What is the worst thing that could happen?"

If you make a gift for someone, they might turn their nose up at it.
If you offer to help someone, they might tell you to go away.
If you smile at someone, they might blank you and not smile back.

And what if you really cared about something, but then you lost it? People move away. Friendships change. Clubs can stop running. Indoor plants can die.

If any of those things happened, you might feel crushed, embarrassed, or sad.

But ninety-nine times out of a hundred, those things don't happen. People love to receive kindness, and giving kindness makes you feel strong and happy.

The benefits are big and the risks are small, so pluck up your courage and dare to care.

## How it helps

When you feel anxious about anything at all, including trying to be caring and kind, the fear can grow bigger even though the risk stays small. That's why it always helps to check from time to time, "What is the worst thing that could happen?"

# Give yourself a gold star

As a person who thinks about kindness and caring, you are good news for the world. You should be proud of yourself.

There are lots of kindness activities in this book. Have you noticed that there is one of these beside each one of them?

Get out your yellow pen or pencil, go back through the pages, and  yourself a gold star for all the kindness activities you have tried.

If you have given yourself any gold stars at all, good for you! Keep up the good work. You can go back anytime and get the ones you missed.

And there is no need to stop when you have them all. You can do them again and again. Being kind and caring, like most things, gets easier the more you do it. Practice makes perfect.

You are a superstar at kindness!

### How it helps

Giving yourself a gold star is a good way of noticing what you have achieved and remembering what you still want to do. Just reading this book is a fantastic start. Give yourself a massive gold star for that!

# For Parents and Carers

Being clear in your thinking about what kindness is
will help you to help your child more effectively.

## What is kindness?

A kind person considers the feelings of others,
tries to help them, and avoids actions that do harm. Affection,
empathy, and giving to others are qualities of a kind person.

## Kindness is natural

Kindness is natural and intuitive. Being able to empathize
and cooperate with each other is an evolutionary advantage
and part of our success as a species. Very young children
will naturally empathize and try and help, even though they
have no expectation of reward.

Everyone has the capacity to be kind. Helping your child doesn't mean trying to
change their personality to make them more sociable and outgoing, but guiding
them to use their natural qualities in ways that contribute to a kinder world.

## Kindness is a strength

It's a tough world, and sometimes parents might feel their children should be tough to cope with it, especially boys. Some people worry that kindness can make children weak. But that is only a danger if we encourage youngsters to help and support others at the expense of their own wellbeing. This has sometimes traditionally been the case with the upbringing of girls.

When self-care is front and foremost, kindness is a type of superpower. It boosts our happiness and self-esteem, and makes us more effective in the world.

## Kindness is a skill

Although kindness is in our nature, it isn't in everybody's experience in equal measure. People who have grown up in environments where kindness was not valued can find it more difficult than others to receive kindness and cultivate it in their own lives.

Shyness, fear of rejection, difficulty in reading the emotions of others, and the feeling that we lack the power to make a difference are some of the things that can get in the way. But the good news is that kindness is a skill we can learn and develop.

# For Parents and Carers

## Why do we want our children to be kind?

Helping children develop their capacity for kindness is not only good for everyone else. It is also hugely beneficial for the child. Research shows that being kind boosts emotional and physical well-being, as well as reducing feelings of isolation and instilling a sense of belonging.

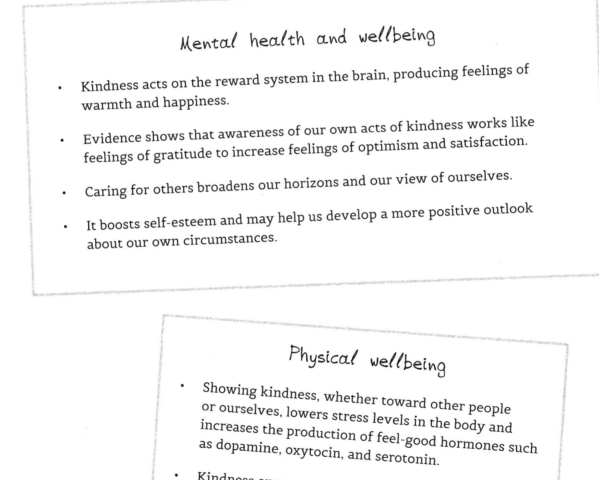

### Mental health and wellbeing

- Kindness acts on the reward system in the brain, producing feelings of warmth and happiness.

- Evidence shows that awareness of our own acts of kindness works like feelings of gratitude to increase feelings of optimism and satisfaction.

- Caring for others broadens our horizons and our view of ourselves.

- It boosts self-esteem and may help us develop a more positive outlook about our own circumstances.

### Physical wellbeing

- Showing kindness, whether toward other people or ourselves, lowers stress levels in the body and increases the production of feel-good hormones such as dopamine, oxytocin, and serotonin.

- Kindness encourages more physical activity. We undertake more exercise when we make an effort on behalf of others as well as ourselves.

## Social wellbeing

- Kindness creates a sense of belonging and reduces feelings of isolation.

- It creates, maintains, and strengthens social connections, building support networks which, in turn, increases self-esteem.

- Empathy and cooperation are linked to likability, more effective. learning and greater success in the workplace

# For Parents and Carers

Helping your child to think about others is an opportunity to bring more kindness into your own life as well as theirs. Here are some ideas about how you can help.

## 1. Let them learn from experience

Acts of kindness are the things we do that are intended to benefit others, and the intention is what matters. Studies show that the benefits to our well-being are lost if we do things for others in anticipation of a reward or because we feel we have to.

Trying to force or shame kids into being nice may control how they behave but miss the benefits. Helping them experience the good feelings that come from caring by giving them plenty of opportunities to be kind means that they will want to do more.

## 2. Talk about it

Talk about kindness. Be clear that other people's feelings matter but not more or less than theirs. Kindness is a choice, and we can build our skills by showing kindness in every area of our lives.

When someone says or does something kind, tell your child about it, particularly how it made you feel. Likewise, don't let acts of unkindness go unremarked upon. Explain why, if someone has said or done something unkind, it was not all right.

## 3. Be part of your community

Being involved with a local community group or supporting initiatives such as free libraries and swap days could give you a great chance to share positive experiences with your child, but even the smallest things, such as contributing to a food bank or stopping to chat with somebody you know will show them that you care about your community.

## 4. Be kind to yourself

Children learn from what you do, not what you say, and they don't miss much. So, show your child what self-care looks like by nurturing your body with good food and exercise and watching what you say about yourself. Don't put yourself down. Even when you don't say negative things about yourself out loud, your body language can give you away.

## 5. Show the "flow"

Encourage your child to find activities they care about enough to give their time and energy to. Share your enthusiasm for your hobbies, though they may not be things that would interest your child. Support their interests as well as you can, even though they might not be things that would interest you.

## 6. Listen

Being able to lend a listening ear, without wading in and trying to solve everything, is one of the skills of kindness. When your child wants to talk, just listen. Let them experience how comforting that can feel, so that they know how to pass it on by listening to other people.

## 7. Make kindness a family value

We live in a culture that doesn't always value kindness, and it's easy not to notice how that can seep into our own attitudes. Comedy on TV often involves laughing at people, on a scale from gentle mockery to downright cruelty. Think about what you watch as a family. News reports usually focus heavily on negative interactions between people: arguments, murders, wars. Could you swap news for something more positive?

Do you tease or use sarcasm—if you said the same words seriously, what would they mean? Children hear things literally. How do you talk about other people behind their back? Are you judgemental? Are you careful to be kind?

## 8. Ask and say thank you

Show your child that it's OK to ask for help. Asking for help gives them opportunities to be kind. If they offer help without being asked, accept it, or at least say thank you for offering. This will help your child feel more confident that they won't be rebuffed if they reach out to others. Thank you messages and letters are a good way to reciprocate kindness.

## 9. Connect and care for the natural world

We call it "Mother Earth" because nature nurtures our well-being. Encourage your child to care about the natural world. Talk about things such as how you can reduce your environmental footprint. Inspire them to care by getting out into nature as much as you can.

## 10. Help them to ask for kindness

If your child asks you for help, you might not always be able to drop everything and pay attention to them, but you can always respond in a caring way. Acknowledge that you have heard them and are glad they asked, and you will help as soon as you are able. Sometimes do a random act of kindness when they haven't asked to show them that they deserve your attention and support whatever is going on in their world.

## 11. Own up to your mistakes, and help them deal with theirs

There is no such thing as perfect kindness, or indeed perfect anything, in this imperfect world. Everything is a work in progress, and you are bound to make mistakes. If you say something hurtful without thinking or upset someone without meaning to, acknowledge it and say sorry. If your child makes a mistake, help them do the same.

## 12. Let them feel their feelings

Let your child feel their feelings. If they are upset because someone has been unkind to them, for example, don't jump straight in and try to distract them or talk them out of it or make things better, because then they won't learn that feelings pass and there is no need to panic.

It isn't about encouraging them to wallow or dwell on difficult emotions, it's about giving them permission to feel the feelings, so they can more easily let them go.

If they are proud of themself and happy, don't burst their bubble. All their feelings matter, and it's only through fully experiencing them that they learn how to manage them. Your job is to accept and acknowledge how they feel in a calm and reassuring way.

### And finally

Helping your child cultivate kindness is good for your child, for you, and for the world. It is also easy, because very small changes in how we think and behave can have wide-reaching effects, like the ripples of a pebble dropped into a pond.

# Glossary

**Albert Einstein**
A famous scientist who was born around 150 years ago in Germany but later settled in America. He was so clever and made such big discoveries that people all over the world have heard of him.

**Benefit**
Something that works for you and makes you feel good.

**Certificate of achievement**
A piece of paper that shows a person has succeeded in something they have been trying to do. It is filled in with their name and often given to them in front of lots of people, such as at a school assembly.

**Chemicals/happiness chemicals**
Everything we can touch, smell, see, and taste is made of chemicals. We have four happiness chemicals in our brains: dopamine, serotonin, oxytocin, and endorphins. They are called happiness chemicals because they get boosted when we do things we enjoy.

**Cocktail stick**
A small wooden stick with sharp points at both ends. It can be stuck through a cherry or other kind of fruit to decorate a drink or make party food easy to pick up.

**Critical**
Pointing out just the bad things.

**Encourage**
Make someone want to do something and help them have the courage to try.

**Fairy tales**
Stories that have been told for many years. They are not always about fairies! They are called "fairy tales" because they often have magical beings like fairies in them.

**Gossip**
Talking about other people when they are not there to hear you.

**Library**
A place where you can borrow books, use a computer, and find out information.

**Organs**
The organs are parts of the body that do specific things. For example, the heart pumps blood, the stomach digests food, and the lungs help us take oxygen from the air to breathe.

**Pen pal**
A friend that you make and keep by writing letters to them.

**Recipe**
Instructions about how to make something.

**Scorched**
Damaged by heat. This might include shrinking, drying out, or having brown marks.

# Further reading

There are lots of great children's books and
online resources about kindness. Here are a few.

## Books

Kindness Is My Superpower: A Children's Book
About Empathy, Kindness and Compassion.
Alicia Ortego

Real Heroes for Boys: True Stories of Courage,
Integrity, Kindness, Empathy, Compassion, and
More! Christy Monson

How Can I Help the World? Inspiring Stories
and Practical Ideas to Help You Join In with
Saving Our Planet. Jenny Alexander

Me and My Feelings: A Kids' Guide
to Understanding and Expressing
Themselves. Vanessa Green Allen

## Online resources

The Kindness Curriculum

https://www.thekindnesscurriculum.com/

Aimed at educators, there are lots of great
ideas here that families can try at home.

World Kindness Movement

https://www.theworldkindnessmovement.org/

## North America

The Random Acts of Kindness Foundation

https://www.randomactsofkindness.org/

Kindness.org

https://kindness.org/about

## UK

Empathy Lab

https://www.empathylab.uk/

## Australia and New Zealand

Care4kids

https://www.careforkids.co.nz/child-care-
articles/article/393/kindness-is-contagious-
create-a-caring-culture

# *Index*